How To Build Massive Arms: 6 Week Workout for Huge Arms, Shocking the Muscles into Growth, Building Massive Triceps, Build Huge Biceps, 20 Mass Building Protein Snacks

Workouts for Muscle Building

By
M Laurence

Table of Contents

Building Big Arms

Building big shirt-busting arms is possibly the number one reason why many of us go to the gym. If it's not THE reason then it's certainly one of our top reasons. Sure big thighs, boulder like calves and breast-plate pecs look great, and certainly get notice, and you should develop them in conjunction with all the muscles of the body if you want the total body. But nothing that gets more attention on a guy than a pair of rippling pythons bulging from the shirt sleeves.

However building size is not as easy as it seems otherwise everyone at the gym would have 20inch guns. Many of us who go to the gym train for hours but don't make the progress we want, if any. Maybe you have hit a plateau, maybe you have just started training or are returning to the gym, or hit a wall where your growth has just stopped and we can't seem to move forward and get that size we crave. That is where this book comes in.

I've written many fitness books, mainly covering overall body development, gaining mass and size, leaning up, on the entirety of the musculature and especially covering diet plans.

With these two key pillars of knowledge I then wanted to write a book that focused on something more specific than overall development. I wanted to get into the fine detail of a specific body part.

I really enjoy training arms, and the more knowledge I have gained, the more research I have learnt, combined with my dietary investigation - led me to pairing down exercises I believe cause the most growth.

This led me to compiling this go-to guide. I certainly didn't want to write a mammoth 300 book that drones on and on for hours. Who has time to read that? There are enough of those about. I wanted to give you a fast 'go-to' guide to 6 weeks' worth of training – the type of book you can throw in your gym bag or have on your phone. Plus I wanted to include a whole selection of easy-to-make snacks and smoothies – pre and post workout nourishment. The type of food and drink that you can make before you go to the gym and when you get back when you're knackered. Fast and simple with a high protein hit to begin the recovery phase as soon as possible.

The next couple of chapters go into some more information regarding training techniques and dietary information to help pack on size. Then we will begin the workouts and ending with 19 high protein snacks and my bonus heavy-duty protein shake.

Optimal Nutrition = Optimal Gains

As we all know building muscle size is a simple combination of hard training and nutrition. Put like that it sounds very easy. To go one step further with nutrition - we must consume more calories than we are burning in a single day - everyday. Otherwise there is no fuel to build additional muscle mass and we will never ever grow size.

Most people know how to workout. Most people know broadly the fundamentals for working each muscle group and allowing rest. But then many of us still struggle with packing on size.

I wanted to focus specifically on building big arms, the kind of arms that draw attention when you're wearing a t-shirt in the supermarket or on the beach. The kind where people come up to you in the gym and ask how you do it.

But it's not just a case of bicep curls, as I would imagine you have probably been doing that. Crucially it's that and much more, it's about more exercises hitting the arms from different angles, it's time on a specific rep, time between sets, intensity and pre-and post-workout nutrition.

Most people fall down on nutrition. This is the first mistake a lot of newbies make when entering the world of muscle building. But not only newbies think they can train harder and still grow even though they aren't consuming enough calories. I've seen many guys who workout for years and make no gains just because they hadn't got their diet plan on point.

Bodybuilding is nutrition. Whether you want an extra two inches on your arms or you want to add 25lbs of overall muscle mass - it is all about the food you ingest.

Improving your arm workout technique is very important – and when to rest is also vital in creating the physique you want, but if your nutrition isn't nailed, it will all be for nothing. My pre and post-workout snacks will help your gains, but you must look at your overall diet too.

However there are a number of other factors you should consider too:

Common Causes of Training Plateaus

- Using the same amount of weight/resistance in each session
- Performing the same exercises in the same order in each session
- Not fully taxing the muscle or working to failure
- Overtraining – not allowing the body enough time to recover. In this book we will train hard enough to rest for a week.

Diet for Huge Arms

To build muscle you need to consume more calories than your body requires to maintain what it has. Every day. Every week. This is a simple concept but not everyone follows it and this can put a dent if not totally stop any type of progress.

What to include?

Your diet should include a mix of protein, carbs and fats. The ratios vary from expert to expert and, but I go for a 40% Protein, 40% Carbs and 20% Fats. These figures can vary body to body. It's up to you to try things out and see how your body reacts.

Some nutritionists say following a solid diet is 50% of building size, others rate it as high as 90%! Yes 90% of what you look like is down to diet, and just 10% weight training. I'd personally say it's more of a 40% training, 60% diet. It's too easy to eat junk after training and use the training to justify it. I've lost count of how many colleagues straight after training go and have pizza and coke plus a protein shake. Are they making progress? Nope!

If we want to build a quality physique, and quality arms, we must be prepared to go all the way.

How much protein do you need?

The RDA is 0.8 grams per kilogram of lean bodyweight (U.S. Food and Nutrition Board, 1980) for sedentary adults (1 kilogram=2.2 pounds)
However you should be aiming for 1.5- 2.4 grams of protein per kilogram of bodyweight. More towards the 2.4 grams will have a maximal effect on building muscle.

So weigh yourself right now - yes now!

Work out now what you should be consuming. Are you consuming enough to sustain your muscle goals? The answer is probably not.

So you need to up your protein intake with each meal and this may mean adding more eggs for breakfast, adding an extra chicken breast for lunch and an extra organic burger or salmon piece for dinner.

Many of the bodybuilders, trainers, and nutritionists agree on these rough figures. Ultimately you will need to find out how your body responds to more protein.

So we haven't even got to the workouts but with this change in your diet going forward you have just made a massive step forward in getting bigger arms. You can now provide the raw materials in which to create the muscle mass.

I've written a couple of books that cover diets for example this one includes a full body workout:

How To Build The Rugby Player Body
https://www.createspace.com/6252083

This book includes quick and easy meals:

Bodybuilding Nutrition: 50 Meals, Snacks and Protein Shakes
https://www.createspace.com/6795960

I wanted to not only include 6 weeks of hardcore workouts, but more importantly a quick reference for pre and post workout nutrition to give you that initial nourishment to kick-start the rebuilding process. You will find 20 recipes for protein shakes and snacks to get you started on and I encourage you to swap out ingredients and get creative to create many more. The critical piece of information is that you need one pre-workout snake/shake before and one after your workout.

Adding a Protein Punch

I'm forever adding a little healthy punch to post-workout meals:

- Adding more whole or egg whites with Breakfast
- Fat Free grated cheese to lunch
- A table spoon of natural Peanut Butter with a protein shake.
- Three table spoons of Cottage Cheese with sliced Beetroot for a slow-release protein in the evening
- Handful of Cashew Nuts as a snack on the go
- Quinoa (contains all six essential amino acids) with Tuna for Lunch
- A Cup of Peas contain around 8 grams of protein

These are just a few easy to add examples to jump up your protein intake.

How To Work Your Arms

Let's just go into how the Biceps and Triceps work so you know exactly how they function.

Biceps Construction

The major action of the biceps brachii is elbow flexion and forearm rotation. The name biceps means that the muscle is made of two heads, a long and a short muscle. These muscle heads have two different origins but come together to form one tendon, which attaches to the radius.

You can feel your biceps working if you place your left hand on your right biceps muscle – let your fingers wrap round your biceps to feel it. Then rotate your Right forearm from a pronated (palm down position) to a supinated (palm up) position. You should feel the muscle flex. You can also feel your biceps work if you put your left hand on your right biceps and flex your elbow – or in other words curl your right biceps with an imaginary weight.

Something to bear in mind is that your biceps can fatigue easily, they are pretty small compared to other muscle groups, and thus relies on your front deltoid and brachioradialis (anterior forearm muscle) for support. So as you can guess once people start to feel their biceps flagging guess what happens? Yep the shoulders take over. So where does that hardcore biceps workout go? Not very far. That's something to always keep in mind. Every rep, every set and every workout. Isolate your biceps, feel them work alone. To maximum size on your arms you must train your mind as much as your muscle.

Triceps Construction

The triceps brachii is named because of its three heads. The triceps is a slightly larger portion of the arm and the triceps main function is to extend the elbow. To feel your triceps, place your left hand on the back of your right arm and then extend your right arm until it is completely straight. If you flex you can feel long and lateral heads of the triceps that create the "horseshoe" shape everyone is striving for. The medial head is mostly covered by the lateral and long heads.

Not all three heads originate at the same place - but they all insert into the elbow. The long head of the triceps originates at the scapula and to isolate it, your elbow must be over your head.

Since the Triceps is bigger than the biceps anyone with large tri's is gonna have a sizeable arm, so these two must be trained as hard as one another.

Now you have a little more information on the muscles themselves, let's get blowing them up!

Arm Workout Week 1

Pre-Workout:
Something with quality carbs and high Protein like my Protein-Packed Oatmeal. Eat that 1 hour before a workout.

We'll start off with this workout designed to totally exhaust the biceps in as short amount of time as possible. People talk about Intensity, I want you to wage war with this workout and indeed all the workouts. I also want you to thoroughly warm up, so do a 5 min run on a machine, 25 star jumps, etc basically get yourself fully warmed up.

I also want you to be fresh for each Biceps and Triceps workout so if you need to split the workouts up, do so – Biceps in the morning, Triceps in the afternoon or on different days. A couple of the workouts are supersets combining both, so no splitting up.

All workouts to be performed once a week. Let's go!

Biceps

Do these 3 exercises one after the other for 1 set, with a 5 second shake out in between. Rest about 2 minutes between the 3 exercise set.

1
EZ BAR CURL
1 sets of 12
Use the EZ Bar and curl the weight up with 1 second blast and lower under a controlled 3 second movement.

Shake out (max 5 seconds) – straight into:

2
INCLINE DUMBBELL CURL
1 sets of 10
Curl with both arms at the same time, supinating your wrists as you go up. Lower the weights slowly - fight it on the way down.

Shake out (max 5 seconds) – straight into:

3
EZ BAR CURL
1 set of 100
Use JUST THE EZ Bar and curl the bar up, once you hit a wall where you can't lift, use your body weight to swing the bar up safely. The KEY part is to control the lowering of the weight – this is where the failure and growth happens.

Triceps
This is the same principle as the Biceps, these 3 exercises equal 1 set - do the sets 3 times. Remember to totally warm up.

1
CLOSE-GRIP BENCH PRESS
1 sets of 12
This exercise is a favourite of many bodybuilders, keep your hands around 8-10 inches apart. Going with a closer grip doesn't put any more stress on your arm, but can add strain on your wrists. Tuck your elbows in to decrease the amount of stress on your pecs and shoulders while increasing the demand on your triceps

Shake out (max 5 seconds) - straight into:

2
TRICEPS PUSHDOWN
1 sets of 12
This is a staple in every triceps workout I do - one of my favs. Keep the body up straight and bend from the elbow only. Allow the arm to come up slightly past perpendicular. This exercise should be done as heavy as possible.

Shake out (max 5 seconds) - straight into:

3
TRICEPS ROPE PUSH-DOWN
1 Set of 100
Low weight, Keep your elbows still and extend arms down. Explosive on the push down, slow and precise on the eccentric (coming up)

Post Workout:

The Mango Shake would be great after this, a sugar hit to raise insulin and 53 grams of protein.

Arm Workout Week 2

Pre-Workout:
Check out the Mexican Black Beans and Avocado

This week we're hitting different parts of the biceps and Triceps and again to be performed once a week. We're reverting to a more standard style of workout. Minimal rests. Just shake outs between sets – no wandering around texting. Get it done.

Biceps

1
REVERSE BARBELL CURL
3 sets of 15 reps
Use the EZ Bar again, curl only from the elbow, keep it strict so you don't use your shoulders to lift the weight. This movement hits my forearms hard

Rest 2 minutes:

2
HAMMER CURLS
3 sets of 12 reps
Hammer Curls
You can be less strict with the form—throw weight around and just burn out those last fibers.

Rest 2 minutes:

3
PREACHER CURL
Dropset to failure
Load a bar with weight you can easily strip. Start with a weight you can hit for 12 reps. Then take off some weight and do as many reps as you can. Take off more weight,

and do it again and again. By the end of this set, your biceps should be pretty much dead.

Triceps
We're hitting these hard today, with volume. But I still only want shake outs between sets. And 2 mins between exercises.

1
TRICEPS PUSHDOWN
4 sets of 12, 8, 8, 8 reps
This is a staple in every triceps workout I do. Keep the body up straight and bend from the elbow only. Allow the arm to come up slightly past perpendicular. This exercise should be done as heavy as possible, including two dropsets.

2
SEATED TRICEPS PRESS
3 sets of 10, 8, 8 reps
This is a serious mass builder for the long head of the triceps. Go as heavy as you can. Don't let your elbows flare. Keep them tucked in tight.

3
LOW CABLE TRICEPS EXTENSION
3 sets of 12, 12, 15 reps
This exercise is similar to a standard dumbbell kick-back, but it keeps the tension on the triceps the entire movement. Be sure to keep the elbow up and to fully extend the arm back. Control the weight back to starting position.

Post Workout:
Try the Chocolate And Banana Shake for a brutal 53 grams of protein.

Arm Workout Week 3

Pre-workout:
Prepare this the night before - Grab-N-Go Protein Hit

Back to being more creative and again once a week. Below is a combined set of 3 exercises that you do with only a shake out in between the time to get to each station. While you have those seconds shake out your arms and go again. Do this 4 times.

Biceps

1
EZ BAR CURL
1 set of 12
Use the EZ Bar and curl the weight up with 1 second blast and lower under a controlled 3 second movement.

Shake out (max 5 seconds) – straight into:

CHIN UP
1 Set until failure
Chin up on a bar and hold for 10 seconds at least. If you can do more, do more until failure.

Shake out (max 5 seconds) – straight into:

EZ BAR CURL
1 set of 12
This time use strict form and lower with 5 seconds – very slow. Keep using strict form until you are forced to use your body to swing the weight up. BUT keep using 5 seconds to lower. This will really burn those fibres.
Rest 2 minutes and go again 4 times.

Triceps

This is a one exercise set, something different to shock the tri's.

1

TRICEPS PUSHDOWN

1 set of 12

Keep the body up straight and bend from the elbow only. Allow the arm to come up slightly past perpendicular. This exercise should be done as heavy as possible.

On the 12th Rep – HOLD for 10 seconds or until total failure.

Shake out arms for 2-3 seconds – THEN:

TRICEPS PUSHDOWN

1 set to total failure

Keep the body up straight and bend from the elbow only. Allow the arm to come up slightly past perpendicular. Keep using strict form until you are forced to use your body to swing the weight up. BUT keep using 5 seconds to lower. This will really burn those fibres.

Repeat 4 more times.

Post-Workout

Try this delicious shake - Choco Peanut Butter Smoothie.

Arm Workout Week 4

Post-Workout:
Try the Iced Breakfast Shake, packed full of carbs and protein and fast to make.

This week we are supersetting Biceps/Triceps for a constant change up, keep the muscles guessing and working really hard. Each set is two exercises, perform each set of Biceps and Triceps one after the other.

Again remember to warm up fully, nothing slows progress like a pulled muscle.

1
EZ BARBELL CURL
4 sets of 5 reps
We are going heavy so you fail on the 5th or 6th Rep. This is stimulating new muscle fibres that are used to the old 8-12 reps. Keep it strict so you don't use your shoulders to lift the weight. Curl only from the elbow.

Just a shake out and then Superset each Set with:

LYING EZ-BAR SKULLCRUSHER
4 sets of 5 reps
Lye on a bench and keep your elbows still and press hard.

2
CABLE SPIDER CURL WITH BARBELL
4 sets of 8 reps
Lye with your chest against an incline bench and curl up the barbell. If you're not familiar with this weight then use a light weight, go for more rep and lighter weight.

Shake out and Superset each Set with:

TRICEPS ROPE PUSH-DOWN
4 sets of 8 Reps
Keep your elbows still and extend arms down.

3
HAMMER CURLS
3 sets to failure
You can be less strict with the form—get the weight up and let it come down using 4 seconds. Just burn out those last fibres.

Shake out and Superset each Set with:

WEIGHTED PARALLEL-BAR DIP
3 sets to failure
Keep your body as vertical as possible—don't lean forward, which hits your chest—and keep those elbows tight to your sides.

Post-Workout:
Try this Almond Blast Shake for a crushing 58 grams of protein.

Arm Workout Week 5

Pre-Workout:
Try my superb Sweet Cinnamon Quinoa Punch.

This changes this up from last weeks heavy-duty load. I'm focusing on high reps. Choose a just the bar at first and see how that feels after 100 reps. If it's too light then choose a weight that just edges up the difficulty but still allows 100 reps.

Biceps

1
BARBELL CURL
1 set of 100 reps
Use just the bar.

Shake it out for 30 seconds

2
TRICEPS PUSHDOWN
1 set of 100
Use the lowest plate weight. This will really burn those fibres.

Shake it out for 30 seconds

3
ALTERNATE DUMBBELL CURLS
100 reps
Use just the dumbbell bars.

Shake it out for 30 seconds

4

WEIGHTED PARALLEL-BAR DIP

As many as possible to failure

Keep your body as vertical as possible—don't lean forward, which hits your chest—and keep those elbows tight to your sides.

5

REVERSE BARBELL CURL

1 set of 100 reps

Use the EZ Bar again, curl only from the elbow, keep it strict so you don't use your shoulders.

Shake it out for 30 seconds

6

CABLE KICK-BACK

1 set to total failure.

A great trick I picked up is to take a bench and incline it up to about 60 degrees – then facing the weight stack with your chest on the bench, you can now perform the cable kick-back with your upper arm locked parallel to the floor.

How do you feel? Still hungry? Go again! Do the full workout again.

Post-Workout:

This will see you right - The Berry Super Shake.

Arm Workout Week 6

Pre-Workout:
For some tasty and fast get this down you - Peppermint Oatmeal Shake

This week will be a mix of heavy loads and 100 reps to totally fatigue the muscles. Are you ready for planet growth?

Biceps

1
EZ BARBELL CURL
5 sets of 5 reps
We are going heavy so you fail on the 5th or 6th Rep. This is stimulating new muscle fibres that are used to the old 8-12 reps. Keep it strict so you don't use your shoulders to lift the weight. Curl only from the elbow.

2
INCLINE DUMBBELL CURL
3 sets of 8, 8, 6 reps
Curl with both arms at the same time, supinating your wrists as you go up. Lower the weights slowly. Go fairly heavy on this movement. As you progress fight it on the way down.

Straight into:

CHIN UP
1 Set until failure
Chin up on a bar and hold for 10 seconds at least. If you can do more, do more until failure.

Straight into:

BARBELL CURL
1 set of 100 reps
Use just the bar.

Done. You should have totally exhausted the biceps if you were really going for it.

Triceps

1

CLOSE-GRIP BENCH PRESS

4 sets of 12, 12, 15 reps

This exercise is a favourite of many bodybuilders, keep your hands around 8-10 inches apart. Going with a closer grip doesn't put any more stress on your arm, but can increase the strain on your wrists. Tuck your elbows in to decrease the amount of stress on your pecs and shoulders while increasing the demand on your triceps.

2

TRICEPS PUSHDOWN

4 sets of 12, 8, 8, 8 reps

This is a staple in every triceps workout I do. Keep the body up straight and bend from the elbow only. Allow the arm to come up slightly past perpendicular. This exercise should be done as heavy as possible, including two dropsets.

On the 12th Rep - HOLD for 10 seconds or until total failure.

Shake out arms for 2-3 seconds - THEN:

3

WEIGHTED PARALLEL-BAR DIP

As many as possible to failure

Keep your body as vertical as possible—don't lean forward, which hits your chest—and keep those elbows tight to your sides.

Post-Workout:
This will ease the pain and taste buds - Chocolate Cherry Shake.

1. Snack - Grab-N-Go Protein Hit

This is a time-efficient Breakfast - prepare the night before - grab and go in the morning with a heavy duty 22 grams of protein.

INGREDIENTS

- 1/4 - cup Rolled Oats
- 1/2 - cup Almond Milk
- 1/2 - scoop Chocolate Protein Powder
- 1 - Large Spoon of Natural Yogurt
- 1 - Banana
- 1 - tbsp Chia Seeds
- 1/2 - tbsp Cinnamon

DIRECTIONS

Mix all ingredients together in a large bowl - slice banana on top and add more Protein powder and Yogurt if additional protein is needed.
Once finished place in plastic container in fridge overnight.

Grab and go in the morning for a fast start to the day.

The easy thing with this is you can take away the oats if you just want a protein hit and this becomes a mid-morning snack. Add more honey to it to spike insulin levels and it becomes the perfect post workout hit.

NUTRITION FACTS

Recipe serves 1
Amount per serving

- Calories 306
- Total Fat 15.6 g
- Total Carb 32.1 g
- Protein 22.7 g

2. Snack- Mocha Pancakes

Coffee Pancakes provide a sure-fire way to rev up your morning workout. The batter can be made the night before and chilled. Whole-wheat pastry flour or spelt flour can be substituted for oat flour.

You can grind up oats into a fine powder which has a denser supply of fibre, vitamins, and minerals than your typical all-purpose flour.

INGREDIENTS

- Oat flour: 3/4 cup
- Plain or vanilla protein powder: 1/4 cup
- Cocoa powder: 2 tbsp
- Cinnamon: 1 tsp
- Baking powder: 1 tsp
- Baking soda: 1/2 tsp
- Large egg: 1
- Strongly brewed coffee (cooled to room temperature): 3/4 cup
- Vanilla extract (omit if using vanilla protein powder): 1 tsp
- Banana, mashed: 1/2 medium
- Hazelnuts or walnuts, chopped: 2 tbsp
- Unsalted butter or coconut oil: 2 tsp
- Raspberries: 1 cup

DIRECTIONS

In a large bowl, stir together the flour, protein powder, cocoa powder, cinnamon, baking powder, baking soda, and a pinch of salt.
In a separate bowl, whisk together the egg, coffee, and vanilla extract. Stir in the mashed banana and nuts.

Add the wet ingredients to the dry ingredients, mix gently, and let the batter rest 15 minutes.
Melt butter or coconut oil in a skillet over medium heat.
Pour 1/4 cup batter for each pancake into the pan, and cook for 2 minutes per side.
Serve the pancakes topped with raspberries, and drizzle them with pure maple syrup if desired.

NUTRITION FACTS

Serving Size: 1/2 recipe, about 4 pancakes
Recipe yields: 2 Servings

- Calories: 425
- Fat: 13 g
- Carbs: 50 g (13 g fibre)
- Protein: 28 g

3. Snack - Protein-Packed Oatmeal

The classic oatmeal breakfast - easy to prepare - excellent slow carbs 29 grams - big on 23 grams of protein with added powder.

INGREDIENTS

- 1/4 - cup Rolled Oats
- 1/4 - cup berries, choose your preference (I used Blueberries)
- 1/2 - cup water - or Oat Milk, Soya Milk, Coconut Milk - you're choice!
- 1/2 - scoop Protein Powder - choose your preference (I usually go for Vanilla)
- 1 - tbsp all-natural Peanut Butter

DIRECTIONS

Place the berries in a microwave-safe bowl and microwave for 30 seconds.
Remove and smash the berries with a fork.
Add oats, water, and protein powder.
Microwave the mixture for 1.30 minutes - then stir - microwave for another 1 minute.

Stir and top with peanut butter if you want even more protein. Or add more protein powder, but it can become a little thick with too much. Also I've found i have to add more water/milk after the first microwave.

In a Saucepan
This does taste better - Add oats and water/milk and protein powder to a saucepan - stir and heat up until it starts to boil. Then leave it for 5 minutes stirring occasionally. Then reheat and serve.

NUTRITION FACTS

Recipe serves 1
Amount per serving

- Calories 317
- Total Fat 12.7 g
- Total Carb 29.4 g
- Protein 23.6 g

4. Snack - Mexican Black Beans and Avocado

Perfect pre-workout snack giving you a hefty 40 grams of carbs.

INGREDIENTS

- 1/2 - cup cooked Brown Rice
- 1/3 - cup cooked Black Beans
- 2 - heaping spoonful's of Salsa
- 1/4 - sliced Avocado
- 2 - tbsp plain Fat-free Greek Yogurt

A hot sauce of your choosing or something like Sweet and Sour - just a dash.

DIRECTIONS

This is ideal if you have ingredients left over. Mix all ingredients in a large bowl - serve and enjoy.

NUTRITION

Serving Size 1
Amount per serving

- Calories 292
- Total Fat 9g
- Total Carbs 40g
- Protein 12g

5. Snack - Fast Yogurt and Apricot

A top-notch evening snack before bed to see you through the night with slow proteins and fats.

INGREDIENTS

- 220 g - of Greek Style Yogurt
- 1-2 - palm-fulls of raw or roasted Almonds (unsalted and unsweetened)
- 1 - palm-full of dried Apricot
- 1 - packet of Stevia (zero calorie sweetener) or a bit of agave or Honey

DIRECTIONS

Mix all the above ingredients in a large bowl - serve in a small bowl and eat up!

NUTRITION FACTS

Serving Size 1
Amount per serving

- Calories 428
- Total Fat 23g
- Total Carbs 31g
- Protein 23g

6. Snack - Protein Banana Smoothie

A stunning protein shake delivering 32 grams of protein.

INGREDIENTS

- 500ml - of Water
- 1 - Scoop of Rice Protein
- 1/2 - Scoop of Pea Protein
- 2 - Bananas
- 0.5 - cup skim milk (OR almond, soy, coconut, or cashew milk)
- 10 - Almonds
- 1 - Handful of Ice

DIRECTIONS

Add all the ingredients to a Blender and mix for 4 minutes. Pour into a shaker for on the go or a tall glass.

Tip - Don't neglect the ice - this really adds to the taste and density.

NUTRITION FACTS

Serving size: 1 shake
Amount per serving

- Calories 320
- Total Fat 8 g
- Total Carbs 32 g
- Protein 32 g

7. Snack - Guacamole Hummus

A great little dish giving you 22 grams of carbs - ideal with a protein shake.

INGREDIENTS

- 1 - can Chickpeas
- 1 - Avocado
- 1 - Jalapeano
- 1/4 - cup chopped cilantro
- Juice from 1 Lime

DIRECTIONS

Mix ingredients together in a large bowl until thoroughly mixed.
Then serve with vegetables, pita chips, or snack of your choice.

Combine with one of the smoothies for more of a protein hit.

NUTRITION FACTS

Serves 4
Amount per serving

- Calories 200
- Total Fat 9 g
- Total Carbs 22 g
- Protein 7.5g

8. Snack - Sweet Cinnamon Quinoa Punch

Walnuts and Quinoa mix to give you a 12grams of protein and 29 grams of carbs.

INGREDIENTS

- 1/4 - cup Quinoa
- 1 - palm-full of Walnuts or Pecans 7-10 individual nuts)
- 1 - palm-full of Blackberries or Blueberries
- Sprinkle of Cinnamon

Sweeten with Stevia (zero-calorie, natural sweetener) or use agave nectar or Honey

DIRECTIONS

Cook your Quinoa in a sauce pan as per instructions on packet. Drain once cooked.
Add the walnuts, blackberries, cinnamon and Stevia and mix it all together with a spoon. Serve hot!

NUTRITION FACTS

Serving Size 1
Amount per serving

- Calories 418
- Total Fat 26g
- Total Carbs 29g
- Protein 12g

9. Snack - Protein Apple and Celery Smoothie

The super shake - 32 grams of protein and 32 grams of carbs - no messing around here.

INGREDIENTS

- 500ml - of Water
- 1 - Scoop of Rice Protein
- 1/2 - Scoop of Pea Protein
- 1 - apple
- 2 - Sticks of Celery
- 0.5 - Cup of skim milk (OR almond, soy, coconut, or cashew milk)
- 10 - Almonds
- 1 - Handful of Ice

DIRECTIONS

Add all the ingredients to a Blender and mix for 4 minutes. Pour into Shaker for on the go or a tall glass.

Tip - Add the ice – it really helps. You could also add a dollop of peanut butter instead of the almonds if you preferred.

NUTRITION FACTS

Serving size: 1 shake
Amount per serving

- Calories 320
- Total Fat 8 g
- Total Carbs 32 g
- Protein 32 g

10. Snack - Peppermint Oatmeal Shake

INGREDIENTS

- 2 scoops chocolate protein
- 1 cup sugar-free vanilla ice cream
- 1 cup oatmeal
- 2 cups nonfat milk
- 1/2 cup water
- 1/2 tsp peppermint extract

DIRECTIONS

Mix all the ingredients together in a blender – and serve! Simple as!

NUTRITION FACTS

Serving size: 1 shake
Amount per serving

- Calories 340
- Total Fat 8 g
- Total Carbs 30 g
- Protein 48 g

11. Snack - Iced Breakfast Shake

Blending whey protein and instant breakfast packs a dual carb and protein hit.

INGREDIENTS

- 1 cup skim milk
- 1 scoop whey protein
- 2 tsp safflower oil
- 1 handful ice
- 1 banana
- 1 package instant breakfast

DIRECTIONS

Mix all the ingredients together in a blender – and serve! Simple as!

NUTRITION

Serving size: 1 shake
Amount per serving

- Calories 270
- Total Fat 12 g
- Total Carbs 30 g
- Protein 28 g

12. Snack - Almond Blast Shake

This protein shake is a brilliant post-workout recovery drink, delivering a solid 58 grams of protein.

INGREDIENTS

- 2 scoops vanilla whey protein
- 1-1/2 cups skim milk
- 1/2 cup dry oatmeal
- 1/2 cup raisins
- 12 slivered almonds
- 1 tbsp peanut butter

DIRECTIONS

Mix all the ingredients together in a blender – and serve! Simple as!

NUTRITION FACTS

Serving size: 1 shake
Amount per serving

- Calories 470
- Total Fat 12 g
- Total Carbs 45 g
- Protein 58 g

13. Snack – The Berry Super Shake

This shake is packed with protein, fibre, healthy fats and probiotics.

INGREDIENTS

- 12 oz water
- 1 cup spinach
- 2 cups frozen mixed berries
- 1/2 cup plain low-fat yogurt
- 2 scoops vanilla protein powder
- 1 tbsp walnuts
- 1 tbsp ground flaxseed

DIRECTIONS

Mix all the ingredients together in a blender – and serve! Simple as!

NUTRITION FACTS

Serving size: 1 shake
Amount per serving

- Calories 500
- Total Fat 11 g
- Total Carbs 54 g
- Protein 57 g

14. Snack – Chocolate And Banana Shake

You'd never guess that a cup of spinach is hiding in this delicious chocolate and peanut butter shake.

INGREDIENTS

1. 12 oz water, milk, or yogurt
2. 2 scoops chocolate flavored protein powder
3. 1 banana
4. 1 cup of spinach
5. 2 tbsp of natural peanut butter
6. 1 tbsp cacao nibs or dark cocoa powder

DIRECTIONS

Mix all the ingredients together in a blender – and serve!

NUTRITION

Serving size: 1 shake
Amount per serving

- Calories 585
- Total Fat 22 g
- Total Carbs 38 g
- Protein 59 g

15. Shake - Chocolate Cherry Shake

INGREDIENTS

- 12 oz water, milk, or yogurt
- 2 scoops chocolate flavored protein powder
- 2 cups of sweet dark cherries, pits removed
- 1 cups of spinach
- 1 tbsp of walnuts
- 1 tbsp ground flax
- 1 tbsp cacao nibs or dark cocoa powder

DIRECTIONS

Mix all the ingredients together in a blender – and serve! Simple as!

NUTRITION FACTS

Serving size: 1 shake
Amount per serving

- Calories 530
- Total Fat 13 g
- Total Carbs 47 g
- Protein 56 g

16. Snack - Superfood Shake

Deeply colored fruits and vegetables like beets and cherries and jammed with healthy nutrients that can boost athletic performance and help muscle recovery.

INGREDIENTS

- 1/2 cup frozen cherries
- 8 oz water
- 1/2 cup chopped raw beets
- 1/2 cup frozen strawberries
- 1/2 cup frozen blueberries
- 1/2 banana
- 1 scoop chocolate whey protein
- 1 tbsp ground flaxseed

DIRECTIONS

Mix all the ingredients together in a blender – and serve! Simple as!

NUTRITION FACTS

Serving size: 1 shake
Amount per serving

- Calories 329
- Total Fat 4 g
- Total Carbs 52 g
- Protein 28 g

17. Snack – The Power Shake

This shake packs 33 grams of healthy protein.

INGREDIENTS

- ¼ cup low fat cottage cheese
- 1 cup blueberries (fresh or frozen)
- 1 scoop vanilla protein powder
- 2 tbsp flaxseed meal
- 2 tbsp walnuts, chopped
- 1½ cups water
- 3 ice cubes

DIRECTIONS

Mix all the ingredients together in a blender – and serve!

NUTRITION FACTS

Serving size: 1 shake
Amount per serving

- Calories 389
- Total Fat 17 g
- Total Carbs 34 g
- Protein 33 g

18. Snacks – Choco Peanut Butter Smoothie

Drink this for the perfect afternoon snack. It's packed with protein, fibre, and antioxidants and peanuts!

INGREDIENTS

- Water as needed
- 2 tbsp flaxmeal
- 1 tbsp unsweetened cocoa powder
- 1 tbsp natural peanut butter
- 1 scoop chocolate whey protein powder

DIRECTIONS

Mix all the ingredients together in a blender – and serve!

NUTRITION FACTS

Serving size: 1 shake
Amount per serving

- Calories 347
- Total Fat 17 g
- Total Carbs 19 g
- Protein 33 g

19. Snack - Mango Shake

53 grams - A high calorie, high impact shake ideal for post or pre workout when you've really killed it with the weights.

INGREDIENTS

- 2 scoops vanilla whey protein powder
- 1 cup frozen chopped mango
- 1 oz of walnuts
- 12 oz orange juice
- Ice as needed

DIRECTIONS

Mix all the ingredients together in a blender – and serve!

NUTRITION FACTS

Serving size: 1 shake
Amount per serving

- Calories 700
- Total Fat 20 g
- Total Carbs 74 g
- Protein 53 g

Bonus - Snack - Summertime Blast

A bonus shake which is high carb hit to replenish lost energy jam-packed with healthy fruits and high vitamin C.

INGREDIENTS

- 2/3 cup seedless watermelon
- 1 scoop of Vanilla Isolate Whey
- 2 tsp lemon juice
- 1/2 cantaloupe
- 1 banana
- 1/4 cup pineapple
- 2/3 cup ice
- 4 to 5 fresh basil leaves

DIRECTIONS

Mix all the ingredients together in a blender – and serve!

NUTRITION

Serving size: 1 shake
Amount per serving

- Calories 182
- Total Fat 1 g
- Total Carbs 47 g
- Protein 28 g

To Kill it – Maximising Gains

How do you really kill it? How do you really maximise your workouts? It's very simple – Dietary Preparation.

One of the biggest mistakes people make is not planning ahead and this is crucial to building muscle mass. Letting your body go without quality fuel will stunt your progress if not completely stop it. There really is no point hammering away in the gym to not provide your body with the right nutrients to grow.

The Big Shop

Firstly you can do a big shop on a Sunday and buy enough food to last until the following Sunday. How much exactly will depend on your nutritional needs. But I'd look at these meals and buy a fair amount and probably more than you need. Once you've done a few shops you'll know exactly what you need. Then you can prepare meals on the Sunday for the next few days so you're not caught short.

3 Day Shop

Another way is to buy enough food to last from Sunday until Wednesday and prepare meals for all those days on the Sunday. Then on the Wednesday I would plan and buy ingredients for Thursday through to Sunday. You will then never find yourself short of key foods to help keep your macro-nutrients at optimal level. Once you've done this a few times it will become second nature and you'll always have the right food to hand.

Something I do now is buy all my fruit and vegetables from the local market. Firstly the prices are much cheaper, and more importantly the quality is superb. It's all fresh and delicious. Plus if you eat eggs you can buy those too from a farmer.

Ordering online means you can purchase most of your food and get it delivered with ease.

So that's the end of my book! I just wanted to thank you for checking out my book and i hope you enjoy the workouts and recipes here.

Please give my book a review, it really helps me and allows me to continue to write useful content for building muscle.

The workouts and recipes are guides for you to experiment with. Remember to warm up properly, also never workout with an injury.

Finally I hope this book helps you with your muscle building gains and while aiding a healthy lifestyle.

-M

How To Build The Rugby Player Body

https://www.smashwords.com/books/view/655303

Made in the USA
Columbia, SC
08 September 2024

42008125R00030